POPE FRANCIS

THE PEOPLE'S PONTIFF

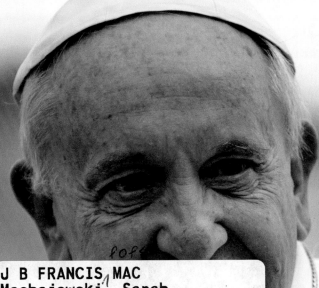

SARAH MACHAJEWSKI

Britannica
Educational Publishing

IN ASSOCIATION WITH

ROSEN
EDUCATIONAL SERVICES

Published in 2015 by Britannica Educational Publishing (a trademark of Encyclopædia Britannica, Inc.) in association with The Rosen Publishing Group, Inc.
29 East 21st Street, New York, NY 10010

Distributed exclusively by Rosen Publishing.
To see additional Britannica Educational Publishing titles, go to rosenpublishing.com.

First Edition

Britannica Educational Publishing
J.E. Luebering: Director, Core Reference Group
Anthony L. Green: Editor, Compton's by Britannica

Rosen Publishing
Hope Lourie Killcoyne: Executive Editor
Andrea Sclarow Paskoff: Editor
Nelson Sá: Art Director
Nelson Sá and Brian Garvey: Designers
Cindy Reiman: Photography Manager
Amy Feinberg: Photo Researcher

Cataloging-in-Publication Data

Machajewski, Sarah.
Pope Francis: the people's pontiff/Sarah Machajewski. — First Edition.
    pages cm — (Making a difference : leaders who are changing the world)
Includes bibliographical references and index.
ISBN 978-1-62275-445-8 (library bound) — ISBN 978-1-62275-447-2 (pbk.) — ISBN 978-1-62275-448-9 (6-pack)
1. Francis, Pope, 1936- I. Title.
BX1378.7.M33 2014
282.092—dc23
[B]

2014004235

Manufactured in the United States of America

Photo credits:
Cover, p. 1 © iStockphoto.com/neneos; cover (inset), pp. 7, 33, 38, 41 Franco Origlia/Getty Images; pp. 3, 6, 16, 26, 34, 43, 44 (background image) Mehmed Zelkovic/Moment Open/Getty Images; pp. 4–5 Filippo Monteforte/AFP/Getty Images; pp. 6–7 Alessandro Bianchi/Reuters/Landov; p. 9 DEA/G. Dagli Orti /De Agostini/Getty Images; pp. 10, 19, 20, 29 © AP Images; p. 14 Emiliano Lasalvia/LatinContent/Getty Images; p. 16 (bottom) Michael Kappeler/picture-alliance/dpa/AP Images; p. 17 L'Osservatore Romano /AP Images; p. 22 De Agostini/Getty Images; p. 27 Jeff J. Mitchell/Getty Images; p. 31 Claudio Peri /EPA/Landov; p. 34 (bottom) Fort Worth Star-Telegram/MCT/Getty Images; p. 36 Charlotte Observer /MCT/Getty Images; cover and interior graphic elements © iStockphoto.com/BeholdingEye (rays), © iStockphoto.com/JSP007 (interior pages border pattern), abstract/Shutterstock.com (silhouetted figures and map).

CONTENTS

INTROD

Pope Francis has been the leader of the Roman Catholic Church for only a short time, but his message of love, peace, and tolerance is already being heard around the world.

The world's population is greater than six billion. About 1.2 billion of those people are Roman Catholic, which means they believe in a certain kind of Christianity. Catholicism is one of the oldest religions in the world. The leader of the Roman Catholic Church is the pope.

For almost two thousand years, different popes have led the church and its followers through some of the most important moments in world history. But in 2013, the Roman Catholic Church experienced an important moment of its own—the election of Pope Francis I.

Pope Francis became the pope in March 2013 when the acting pope at the time, Benedict XVI, stepped down from his position. Since then, Francis has become known for reaching out to the poor and helping people in need. Above all, he is known for being compassionate. His behavior is quite different from that of previous popes, which makes many people excited for the church's future.

Though he hasn't been pope for long, Francis is already changing the church—and the world—for the better. As one of the world's most visible spiritual leaders, the new pope has the opportunity to make changes that will affect millions of people.

CHAPTER 1

A Future Leader Is Born

The pope was born in Buenos Aires on December 17, 1936. Buenos Aires is the capital of Argentina, a country in South America. His father came to Buenos Aires from Italy. His mother was born and raised in Buenos Aires. Together, they had five children. Though the world knows the pope as Francis, his birth name was Jorge Mario Bergoglio.

A Religious Youth

Jorge grew up in a traditional household. His parents were devout Catholics. They raised their children to believe in Catholicism, too. Religion was

Bergoglio became the pope at the age of seventy-six, after a lifetime of dedication to his faith and the church.

A young Bergoglio, standing second from the left, is seen here with his family in Argentina.

an important part of the Bergoglio children's upbringing, and Jorge and his brothers and sisters attended Catholic schools. Jorge graduated from a Catholic high school with a chemical technician's diploma. He worked as a laboratory technician for a few years after that.

Bergoglio spent a few years in the secular world, but he felt a calling to the church.

He believed that devoting his life to God was what he was meant to do. In 1955, he began studies at a seminary in Buenos Aires. In 1958, he began a novitiate to become a Jesuit, or a member of the Society of Jesus. A novitiate is the period of training and preparation a person must go through before becoming a full member of a religious order.

While going through his novitiate, Bergoglio studied humanities at a school in Santiago, Chile. Then he earned a licentiate (similar to a master's degree) in philosophy in Buenos Aires. After he graduated, he taught literature and psychology to high school students. He

QUICK FACT

After high school, Bergoglio became ill with life-threatening pneumonia. He even had part of his lung removed. This was the only serious health crisis in his life, which made him a good candidate for pope in his later years.

also used this time to work toward yet another degree. This time, the subject was theology, the study of religion.

Bergoglio's interest in education is very much in line with the Jesuits' beliefs. The Society of Jesus is known for its educational,

A Spanish knight named Ignatius of Loyola founded the Society of Jesus in the sixteenth century.

missionary, and charitable works. Its interest in education and charity has helped modernize the Catholic Church over the years. Not coincidentally, Pope Francis—the first Jesuit pope—has already been credited with modernizing the current church.

A Priest with a Purpose

Bergoglio was ordained as a priest in 1969. He took his final vows in the Jesuit order in 1973. Bergoglio could have remained a priest, but he took on leadership roles within the Jesuit sect of Argentina's Catholic Church. A year after taking

This 2003 photo shows the pope, then known as Cardinal Bergoglio, carrying out his religious duties among the people of Argentina.

QUICK FACT

Cardinals are senior officials within the church who elect the new pope. Francis helped elect Pope Benedict XVI, whom he later replaced in 2013.

his vows, he became the head of Argentina's Jesuits. He was their leader for six years.

In 1992, Bergoglio became the auxiliary bishop of Buenos Aires, which means he was second-in-command to the archbishop. Then, in 1998, he was named the archbishop of Buenos Aires. He became a cardinal in 2001 and kept this title until he was elected pope.

Bergoglio used his positions as auxiliary bishop and archbishop to begin his most meaningful work: advocating for the poor. He believes that it is the church's job to assist people who need help the most, as this is a value upon which the Catholic Church was founded. He has even told reporters that he would like to see "a poor church, and [a church] for the poor."

As archbishop, Bergoglio focused on sending priests to reach the people in Argentina's slums, or poorest neighborhoods. Under his leadership, the number of priests sent to these areas more than doubled. This work not only helped people in need, but it also showed that the Catholic Church made it a priority to help others. His actions as archbishop showed the world that the church could and would make a difference for those in need. It also demonstrated his personal values.

A COMMITMENT TO HIS PEOPLE

Bergoglio reached all of his positions in Argentina through hard work and commitment to his faith. Along the way, he began gaining a reputation for humility. As a Catholic leader in a religious country, he could have lived comfortably using the church's money. He chose to live simply instead.

It didn't take long for people to notice this. It became most apparent because of his

Bergoglio restructured the Argentinean Catholic Church's bank accounts and spending policies. He believed the church was meant to help people in need—not to spend money on itself.

actions during the economic crisis in Argentina in the 1990s. The country's economy collapsed, and its currency (the peso) became worth very little. Many people suffered financially as a result. In response, Bergoglio decided to live in an ordinary apartment in Buenos Aires instead of the home in which the city's archbishop usually lived. He also used public transportation, preferring to take the bus or walk rather than travel in expensive cars. This public display of humility made people feel as if he were one of them during a difficult time.

Bergoglio lived a simple, humble life despite being Argentina's most important religious leader. Here, he is seen taking public transportation even though private cars were available to him.

Bergoglio's reputation for living modestly among the people has stayed with him throughout his entire career, all the way to the world's stage as pope.

A COMMITMENT TO HIS BELIEFS

As archbishop, Bergoglio held conservative beliefs about social issues. That means he believed that people should follow traditional ways of life. These beliefs often caused him to be at odds with the government of Argentina. He was outspoken about his disapproval of the government's decisions, especially when they conflicted with the Catholic Church's beliefs.

Taking on Argentina's government sometimes created tension, especially because its leaders were popular. However, Bergoglio didn't let that keep him quiet. His determination proved that he was a strong leader who was capable of standing up for his and his people's beliefs. These qualities set him apart from his peers and colleagues and helped him when a once-in-a-lifetime opportunity came along: a chance to become the pope.

C ardinal Bergoglio became pope in 2013 under unusual circumstances. Typically, a new pope is elected only after the current pope dies. However, on February 11, Pope Benedict XVI announced that he was resigning from office because of ill health. He would step down at the end of the month. Benedict was the first pope to resign since Pope Gregory XII in 1415. Every other pope since Gregory

Francis I waves to the public from the balcony of St. Peter's Basilica after being elected as the new pope.

had served until he died.

The church's cardinals found themselves in the unexpected situation of having to elect a new pope. On March 12, they came together in the Sistine Chapel in Rome, where they held a conclave. At this kind of meeting, the cardinals meet privately

Cardinals attend a mass at St. Peter's Basilica in preparation of electing a new pope.

behind closed doors until they make a decision. They take a vow of secrecy during this time and cannot reveal anything to the outside world. A tradition is followed to use smoke from the chapel chimney to indicate whether a decision has been made. Black smoke means there has been no decision, whereas white smoke is the signal that a new pope has been elected.

When the white smoke rose from the Sistine Chapel on March 13, it was to let the world know that Cardinal Jorge Bergoglio from Argentina was now Pope Francis I. He was the first pope from the Americas and the first Jesuit pope.

WHAT DOES THE POPE DO?

The pope rules the church, much as a king rules a country. He has an organization called the Roman Curia to help him. The pope decides the church's position on issues. He has the power to call general meetings that determine church policy. The pope also appoints bishops and assigns them to regions called dioceses.

The pope himself is the bishop of Rome, Italy. He rules Vatican City, which lies within Rome's borders but is a separate country. Vatican City is all that remains of the Papal States, a region of Italy that the popes ruled from 756 to 1870 CE.

The pope is not only the most powerful man within the Roman Catholic Church but also the leader of all Catholics. It's a leadership position on a very public stage. Millions of people watch the pope's actions because he represents the church. In the past, popes have been criticized for being too strict, old-fashioned, or out of touch with modern society. The surprise election in 2013 was an opportunity for the church to choose a leader who could change this opinion. That leader was Pope Francis.

People from all over the world gathered in St. Peter's Square, seen in this photo, to witness the announcement of the new pope.

WHY BERGOGLIO?

Jorge Bergoglio was elected pope because his work in Argentina proved he could be a successful leader. He was committed to his faith, and he showed he could turn those values into action. These actions made positive differences in people's lives. His work with Argentina's

Onlookers in St. Peter's Square celebrate with a Vatican flag upon hearing that a new pope had been elected. They would soon find out that their new leader was Pope Francis I.

Pope Francis lives in the Vatican guesthouse instead of the official papal residence in the Apostolic Place. The guesthouse allows him to receive visitors and hold meetings.

poor showed his dedication to Catholicism's charitable roots. Successfully managing the Argentinean church's money showed he could run an organization well. Finally, he was the most powerful religious leader in a country with a great number of Catholics. Argentina, like most South American countries, has a large Catholic population. Electing a pope from this part of the world, rather than from Europe, was a way to strengthen the church's ties to many of its followers. All of these reasons made Bergoglio a strong candidate for being chosen pope. On March 13, 2013, when news broke that he was elected, the world celebrated the news from the Vatican.

What's In A Name?

Everything Bergoglio did from the moment he was elected demonstrated his commitment to turning around the public's opinion of the Roman Catholic Church, which had suffered in recent years due to scandals. Even the papal name he chose reflected his dedication to helping those in need. He chose Francis, after Saint Francis of Assisi, who was known for his concern for the well-being of the poor. Bergoglio had always admired how St. Francis influenced the church to care for the poor and to be

St. Francis of Assisi lived a life of poverty and devoted his life to helping the poor. Bergoglio admired his message and chose his papal name in honor of the saint.

Some cardinals suggested that Pope Francis should have taken the name "Adrian" after Pope Adrian VI, who was known as a reformer of the church.

less concerned with material goods. As pope, he wanted to lead by the same kind of example.

Choosing this name, then, ended up being symbolic: it was a message to people who believed the church was too traditional, too set in its ways, and too concerned with money. When Francis was elected, people recognized the value he placed on living simply and helping the poor. Many Catholics hoped having Francis as the church's leader would be an opportunity for the church to practice these values again. It was almost as if history was repeating itself within the church, but this time, it was with a different Francis.

Pope Francis addressed the world for the first time by saying "good evening." Using such an informal phrase showed the world he wanted to be viewed as a regular person.

Off to a Good Start

Pope Francis, from the day of his election, was determined to make changes that would benefit both the church and people around the world. He knew his new position made him highly visible to the world and that all of his actions would be watched closely.

The day the pope is elected is an important day. Thousands of people gather in St. Peter's Square to watch the new pope greet followers from the Vatican's balcony. This ritual involves many customs, right down to what the pope wears. Normally, he wears traditional papal robes and a large hat. Pope Francis chose to wear simple white robes instead. He also put on the iron cross he had worn as archbishop instead of the gold one given to popes. It shocked people, but in a good way. There were even reports that his assistants inside of the church were shocked, too. But that hadn't stopped Francis before. Once again, he was committed to his values, even if it meant defying many centuries of tradition.

As the day's activities wore on, Pope Francis continued to demonstrate his humility. He chose to stand and greet each cardinal individually to receive his congratulations, rather than sitting on the papal throne. Later that evening, he declined to take the fancy car that was waiting to take him from the Vatican to churches around Rome. Instead, he rode in a minibus with the other bishops and cardinals.

Pope Francis's actions showed he didn't want all the fuss, attention, and expenses that are normally lavished on the pope. In just one short day, Francis was already making a difference in the Catholic and world community.

CHAPTER 3

THE COMPASSIONATE POPE FRANCIS

Pope Francis is the most visible spiritual leader in the world. Many spiritual leaders teach a message of love, compassion, and tolerance. Pope Francis is one leader who not only preaches this message, but lives it, too. He upholds the church's fundamental beliefs, cares for the poor, and truly seems to enjoy interacting with the common people.

A SIMPLE MESSAGE

Pope Francis's message is simple and direct. It is easy to say and think that love, compassion, and tolerance are good. However, it's sometimes hard to practice these values on a daily basis. This is true for the average person. Imagine having to live that message every day in front of millions of people! That's what Pope Francis does. As the pope, the world watches all of his actions closely. While this may seem like a great deal of pressure, Pope Francis has embraced his role. He sees his position as an opportunity to

Pope Francis greets onlookers in St. Peter's Square after a mass in March 2013.

lead millions of people by example. By showing how to love others and be compassionate, he can inspire others to do the same.

These regular acts of love and compassion began when Francis was a religious leader in Argentina. He helped Argentina's poorest citizens because he felt they needed the most attention and care. His way of helping the poor was to send more priests to their neighborhoods to talk with them, pray with them, and provide support. During mass, Francis often preached to listeners about the importance of helping the poor.

LEADING BY EXAMPLE

Francis paid much attention to helping Argentina's sick and needy. He not only sent

QUICK FACT

Pope Francis has a very popular Twitter account. In December 2013, he had over 3.3 million followers.

priests to reach out to them, but he also did it himself. He made it a tradition to spend every Holy Thursday (the Thursday before Easter) washing the feet of people in need. It became a ritual for him to wash the feet of people in jails, hospitals, and nursing homes.

The ritual of washing someone's feet is very symbolic to Catholics. In ancient times,

This photo shows Pope Francis washing and kissing the feet of a young man during a mass for troubled youth in Buenos Aires.

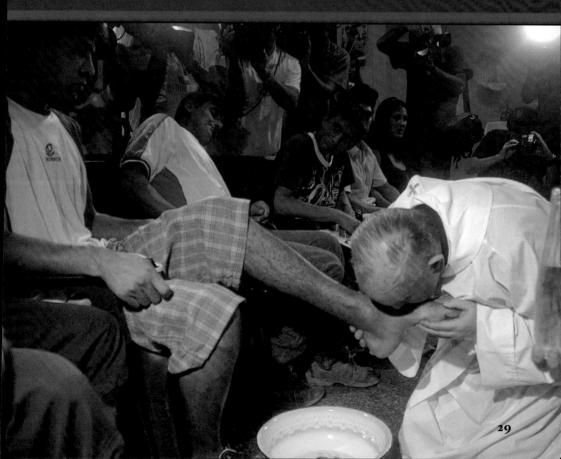

foot washing was something servants did for their masters and their guests. It was an act of hospitality but also one of servitude. However, Catholics believe that Jesus Christ washed the feet of his twelve apostles on the evening of the Last Supper. The act came to be viewed as one of humility and kindness.

Francis continued this tradition on his first Holy Thursday as pope, washing the feet of twelve inmates in a youth prison. People don't normally expect the powerful to interact with the common people, which made his actions even more touching—and surprising. But Pope Francis wanted make the needy feel better, even if it was just for a short moment.

Just as he did in Argentina, the pope regularly performs acts of charity and kindness. By

QUICK FACT

Pope Francis has washed the feet of women, Muslims, and Jews, in addition to Catholic men. This has surprised many people, but the pope has made an effort to treat everyone as equals.

touching the lives of the most disadvantaged, Francis proves that compassion can truly make a difference in the world.

WEEKLY ACTS OF KINDNESS

Every Wednesday, Pope Francis delivers an address in St. Peter's Square in Vatican City. Thousands of people gather to hear the pope's weekly sermon. He sets aside time afterward to greet sick or disabled people who have gathered in the square. Pope Francis embraces them and gives them a personal blessing.

Pope Francis embraces a man with a tumor disorder. This compassionate act went viral on the Internet in November 2013, with people around the world seeing Francis's message of love.

Francis has done this every week since becoming Pope, and he has made headlines several times for extraordinary acts of compassion. In November 2013 alone, he twice embraced severely disfigured men in front of crowds of about fifty thousand people. He drew them close to his chest and spoke kind words to them. Images of these acts of kindness went viral on the Internet. In a matter of hours, the entire world saw what Pope Francis had done.

Francis received an incredible amount of praise and support for his simple actions. However, he didn't do these things for praise or attention. He was simply living the message of love and kindness that he preaches.

QUICK FACT

The pope has become known for his kindness toward children. When they interrupt his sermons, he hugs them and speaks to them kindly, rather than getting angry.

Each time the pope does something like this, it becomes an opportunity to make a difference in the world. There's a chance people may change their behavior after seeing what the pope does. For example, the next time they see a person in need on the

Pope Francis carries on with his mass, and with a smile, despite being interrupted for a hug.

street, they may remember Pope Francis and stop to be kind to him or her. Pope Francis's simple acts set an example that, if followed, can change the world.

Pope Francis's actions during his life have made him seem like a simple, loving man. His beliefs closely match the ideals that the Roman Catholic Church was founded upon.

In recent years, though, the Catholic Church has had problems with its image. It appeared to be very strict and conservative. Many people thought it was out of touch with modern values. People's lives had changed,

The Catholic Church's reputation has suffered in recent years because of its strict beliefs and hesitation to accept different lifestyle choices.

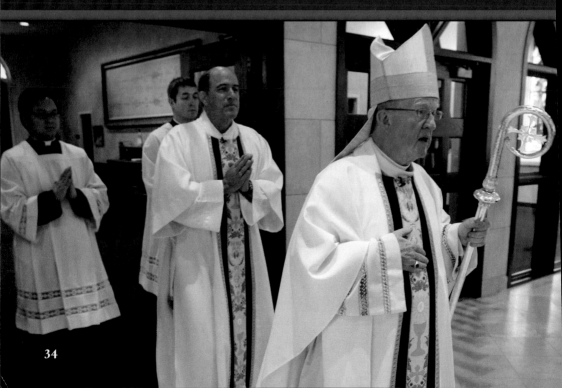

and their lifestyles didn't always match what the church taught. The amount of money the church had and spent also created a divide between it and its followers. The church risked becoming known as an old institution that would no longer be as influential in people's lives as it was in the past.

The church, instead of embracing society's changes, held steadfastly to its beliefs. Popes and priests spoke against certain lifestyles, such as those of divorced people, unmarried parents, and gay people. Many people felt unwelcome in the Catholic Church because of how they lived. So they left. Others left the church to support their friends or family members whom they felt were not welcome in the church. This

QUICK FACT

Pope Francis's open-mindedness comes from decades of hands-on work with people. He's had to work to find ways to translate the church's beliefs for the real world.

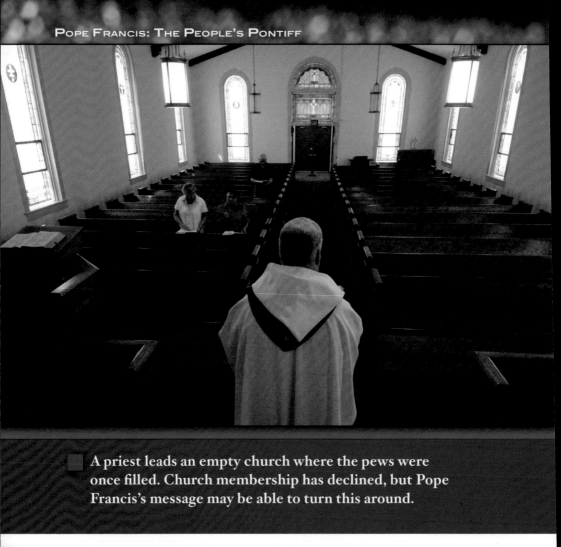

A priest leads an empty church where the pews were once filled. Church membership has declined, but Pope Francis's message may be able to turn this around.

caused the church's membership numbers to decline. Blame for this was often placed on the pope.

When he took his new position, Pope Francis was faced with a choice. Should he continue this strict mind-set, which pushed many people away, or should he lead the church in a new, accepting direction? So far, he has chosen the second option.

A More Tolerant Church

Pope Francis likely hasn't been pope long enough to make long-lasting changes, but he is certainly off to a good start. He has begun the process of changing the church by having an open dialogue with his followers. That means he wants to talk about these issues publicly.

The pope is very used to speaking and listening to others. His experience as a religious leader has made him comfortable delivering messages to large groups of people.

Quick Fact

In 2013, Pope Francis sent a survey to Catholic priests. It asked them questions such as how many divorced families attended their church and if there were any gay members. He did this to get an idea of what modern Catholics are like.

Now he just does this on a bigger scale because he is the pope.

One of the first issues the pope has decided to tackle through conversation is the church's opinion of gay people. This topic has always been controversial, but it has come to the forefront in recent years. Much of society, especially the younger

The pope's message of tolerance is drawing the attention and support of groups of people who have been rejected by the church in the past.

In 2010, Francis (then archbishop) argued that the Argentinean Catholic Church should support civil unions between gay people. This showed he was willing to compromise between the church's beliefs and modern lifestyles.

generation, has moved toward greater acceptance of gay people. Many states in the United States now allow same-sex marriage, and the number of people who lead an openly gay lifestyle has increased.

Despite these societal changes, the Roman Catholic Church has remained opposed. The church does not approve of homosexuality because of what the Bible says. As a result, the church's policies and teachings on this subject have made many gay people feel judged and attacked.

Pope Francis's attitude is that every gay person should be treated with respect and love. In one of his most famous quotes to date, Pope Francis told reporters, "If a person is gay and seeks God and has good will, who am I to judge them?"

This attitude sent shockwaves throughout the religious and world community. For the first time in the history of the Roman Catholic Church, its leader finally said something positive about gay people. Members of the gay community finally felt that someone was on their side. However, many older Catholics and Catholic leaders were angered by the pope's tolerant remarks. They publicly criticized the new pope, arguing that his statement went against the church's beliefs.

This isn't the first time Francis has faced criticism. Rabbi Abraham Skorka of Argentina said his friend dealt with many pressures as archbishop of Buenos Aires. Skorka told reporters, "The criticism he is suffering from is not new for him....He's a very strong man and he will go ahead."

This street art mural in Rome shows Pope Francis as a superhero. Will he live up to expectations? Only time will tell.

A Leader for All

As the top spokesman for the church, Pope Francis's message is that God loves everyone, and, therefore, it is wrong for the church to turn anybody away. The pope's commitment to his values and beliefs has impressed millions of people. He is quietly leading by example and preaching a message of love and acceptance.

Pope Francis believes that if people experience the church's kindness, they can lead a more fulfilled life. They may even change their own behavior for the better. In this way, Pope Francis's leadership has the power to make the world a better place.

December 17, 1936 Jorge Mario Bergoglio is born in Buenos Aires, Argentina.

1955 Bergoglio begins studies at a seminary in Argentina.

1958 Bergoglio enters a Jesuit novitiate.

1969 Bergoglio is ordained as a priest.

1973 Bergoglio takes his final vows in the Jesuit order.

July 1973 Bergoglio becomes the head of Argentina's Jesuits, an office he holds for six years.

March 1986 Bergoglio finishes his doctoral thesis in Germany.

1992 Bergoglio becomes the auxiliary bishop of Buenos Aires.

1998 Bergoglio becomes the archbishop of Buenos Aires.

2001 Bergoglio is appointed a cardinal of the Catholic Church.

April 2005 Pope John Paul II dies. A conclave elects Pope Benedict XVI as the new pope. It is rumored that Cardinal Jorge Bergoglio from Argentina received the second-highest number of votes.

February 11, 2013 Pope Benedict announces he will resign as pope.

March 13, 2013 Bergoglio is elected pope. He takes the name Francis I.

December 2013 *Time* magazine chooses Pope Francis as its "Person of the Year" for "pulling the papacy out of the palace and into the streets, for committing the world's largest church to confronting its deepest needs, and for balancing judgment with mercy."

- Martin Luther King Jr. Martin Luther King Jr. was an activist and religious leader who fought for equal rights for African Americans in the 1960s. His peaceful example became the face of the civil rights movement and helped effect change in the United States. He received the Nobel Peace Prize in 1964.
- Dalai Lama The Dalai Lama is a Buddhist leader in Tibet. The current Dalai Lama is an advocate for Tibetans and promotes a message of compassion, nonviolence, and peace.
- Mother Teresa Mother Teresa was a Catholic nun who dedicated her life to helping the poor, sick, and needy. Admired and respected by many, she won the Nobel Peace Prize in 1979.
- Pope John Paul II Pope John Paul II was the 264th pope and a respected religious leader. He significantly improved relations between Catholics and people of other faiths.
- Desmond Tutu Desmond Tutu is a social rights activist from South Africa. An Anglican bishop and archbishop, he fought for equal rights for blacks in South Africa in the 1980s. He won the Nobel Peace Prize in 1984. Today, he speaks out against poverty, racism, and sexism.

advocate To argue for or support a cause or policy.

archbishop The chief bishop responsible for a district of people.

auxiliary Supporting.

civil union A legally recognized union of a same-sex couple.

compassion Awareness of the suffering or misfortune of another, together with a desire to help the person.

conclave A private meeting in which cardinals of the Roman Catholic Church elect a new pope.

defy To go against or resist.

devout Having or showing deep religious commitment.

hospitality Generous and friendly treatment of visitors and guests.

humility The quality or state of being humble.

material Concerned with physical rather than spiritual needs.

ordain To make a person a priest by a special ceremony.

sect A religious body within a larger group, consisting of members having similar beliefs.

secular Not religious.

seminary A college that prepares students to be priests, ministers, or rabbis.

sermon A talk on a religious or moral subject.

servitude The state of being a slave or subject to the control of a more powerful person.

spiritual Of or relating to sacred or religious matters.

Books

Gerner, Katy. *Catholicism* (Religions Around the World). New York, NY: Marshall Cavendish Benchmark, 2009.

Lanser, Amanda. *Pope Francis: Spiritual Leader and Voice of the Poor* (Essential Lives). Minneapolis, MN: ABDO Publishing Company, 2014.

Rubin, Sergio, and Francesca Ambrogetti. *Pope Francis: Conversations with Jorge Bergoglio*. New York, NY: G. P. Putnam's Sons, 2013.

Watson, Stephanie. *Pope Francis: First Pope from the Americas* (Gateway Biographies). Minneapolis, MN: Lerner Publications Company, 2014.

Whitbread, Henry. *Lives of the Great Spiritual Leaders*. New York, NY: Thames & Hudson, 2011.

Websites

Because of the changing nature of Internet links, Rosen Publishing has developed an online list of websites related to the subject of this book. This site is updated regularly. Please use this link to access the list:

http://www.rosenlinks.com/mad/fran